Tenor Banjo Christmas Solos

Classic Christmas Melodies in New Settings for the Tenor Banjo

Rob MacKillop

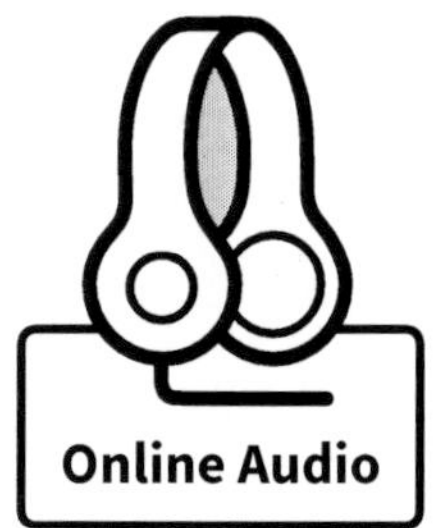

To access the online audio recording go to:
WWW.MELBAY.COM/30994MEB

The Deering Eagle II 19-Fret Tenor Banjo on the cover is courtesy of Deering Banjo Company.

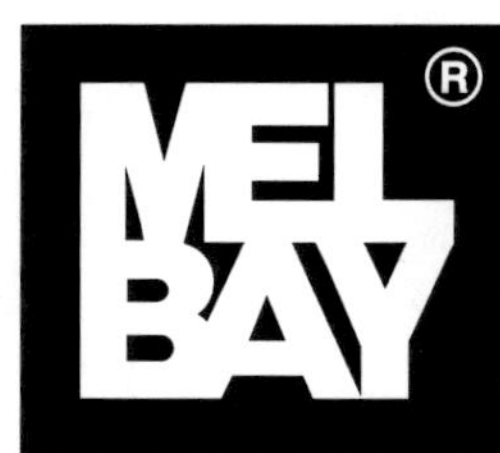

WWW.MELBAY.COM

INTRODUCTION

This book counters the claim that, "The Devil gets all the best tunes!"

In making my arrangements of these classic seasonal tunes, I have tried to colour them in chord-melody style with jazz chords, folk influences, classical elements, engaging instrumental voice lines underneath the melody, and more.

Not only are they enjoyable to play and hear, but for many – your technique will be enhanced at the same time. I teach a variety of fretted instruments, and in my Mel Bay books I always try to develop the musician as much as his or her technique. Analyse as best you can what is going on musically. Try different fingerings, explore tonal contrasts, and greater dynamic changes from very quiet to very loud, intimate to strident.

If you need help, drop me a line through my website, RobMacKillop.net. I teach many students internationally via Zoom, and I would be happy to assist you.

Rob MacKillop
South Queensferry
Edinburgh
2021

CONTENTS

Commentary

Away in a Manger - We start with a very simple arrangement of a beautiful melody known more in Europe than America, but one which I'm sure you'll love. The melody repeats from the last beat of measure 9, but the arrangement gets busier, increasing in tension a little before calm returns in the last line.

Silent Night - Another fairly simple setting, with echoing parts in different registers. Lots of standard chord shapes are used, mainly in four parts, so try to figure out the chords you are playing. If that is beyond you, don't worry as the Mel Bay website has many tenor-banjo books to help you.

Auld Lang Syne - The musical language is more advanced here, as I wrote it in homage to the great jazz tenor-banjo player, Eddy Davis, The Manhattan Minstrel, who sadly left us in 2020. Note the instruction to play "Slowly, tenderly, reflective". The second chord in the first full measure, G with a ♭5 in the bass, is correct. If you think it sounds odd, play it many times over until it sounds just right! Think of such odd notes as *colours*, potentially revealing deeply felt emotional states.

Ding Dong Merrily on High - The first eight bars provide exercise in playing the interval of the 6th on the inner two strings. Start slowly until you have all the notes confidently under your fingers, then increase the speed to suit your interpretation of the song. Measures 9 to 14 have shifting chords over a C and G drone on the lower strings. Try not to lose control of the strings here.

O Christmas Tree - This arrangement starts conservatively, but look out for the running chromatic lower voice from measure 10.

I Saw Three Ships - Another drone here, based this time on a G chord. Note the dynamic changes for the first time through the first page. Try to emphasise the melody through measures 18 to 25. Measures 26 to 33 give you more opportunity to practise 6ths. Finally, strum through the first page again – ignoring the quiet dynamic marking – for a finale.

In the Bleak Midwinter - A two-part arrangement, the A section being largely in chord-melody style, the B section with a more or less constant run of eighth notes. Be sure to extract the melody, indicated with accent marks, in the B section.

The Coventry Carol - This medieval carol has a number of interesting challenges. Note the number of time signatures. Try to keep a fairly steady, but not metronomic, beat throughout. The first page has some long stretches for the left hand, which might be too much for some players. But don't worry: the second page has the same music with slight changes to make it easier to play. I wrote it out with three-voice chords, as modern tenor-banjo playing – even in jazz – has moved away from the fairly constant usage of four-part chords favoured in the past.

Once in Royal David's City - Less well known in the US than the UK and elsewhere, this was my favourite song to sing in primary school. Watch out for the two-note chords in measures 12 and 16.

What Child Is This? - Better known in the UK as "Greensleeves", and once thought to be composed by Henry VIII.

Four Medieval Pieces - As a break from the traditional Christmas tunes, I thought I would include some pieces devoted to Mary and Jesus from earlier times and places. Although technically quite straightforward, these pieces do have some unusual rhythms, which will take some careful counting. The Catalan pieces "Cuncti Simus" and "Los Sept Goyts" are from the *Libre Vermell de Montserrat*, the Spanish "Rosa das rosas" from the *Cantigas de Santa Maria*, and finally the Finnish/Swedish "Gaudete" is from *Pia Cantiones* of 1581, arguably more a Renaissance piece, despite its characteristically medieval sound. I highly recommend the editions by Gaita for authentic transcriptions from original sources of medieval music.

Recording Equipment
Rode NT4 stereo mic into a Fostex FR2LE hard-disk recorder.

Instrument
Deering Sierra tenor banjo with Thomastik-Infeld flat-wound strings [10/15/21/31]

Away in a Manger

Arranged by
Rob MacKillop

W. J. Kirkpatrick

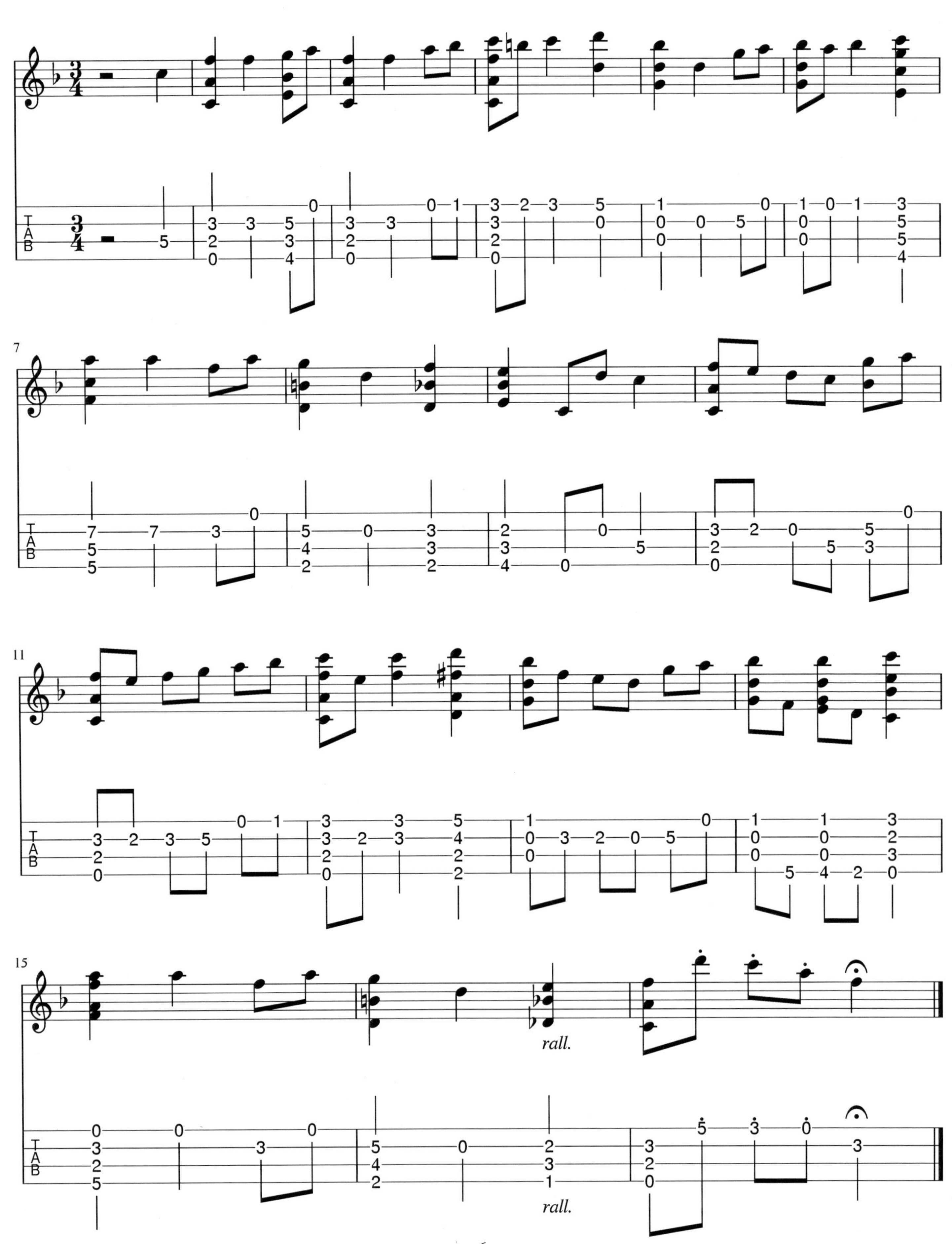

Silent Night

Arranged by
Rob MacKillop

F. Gruber

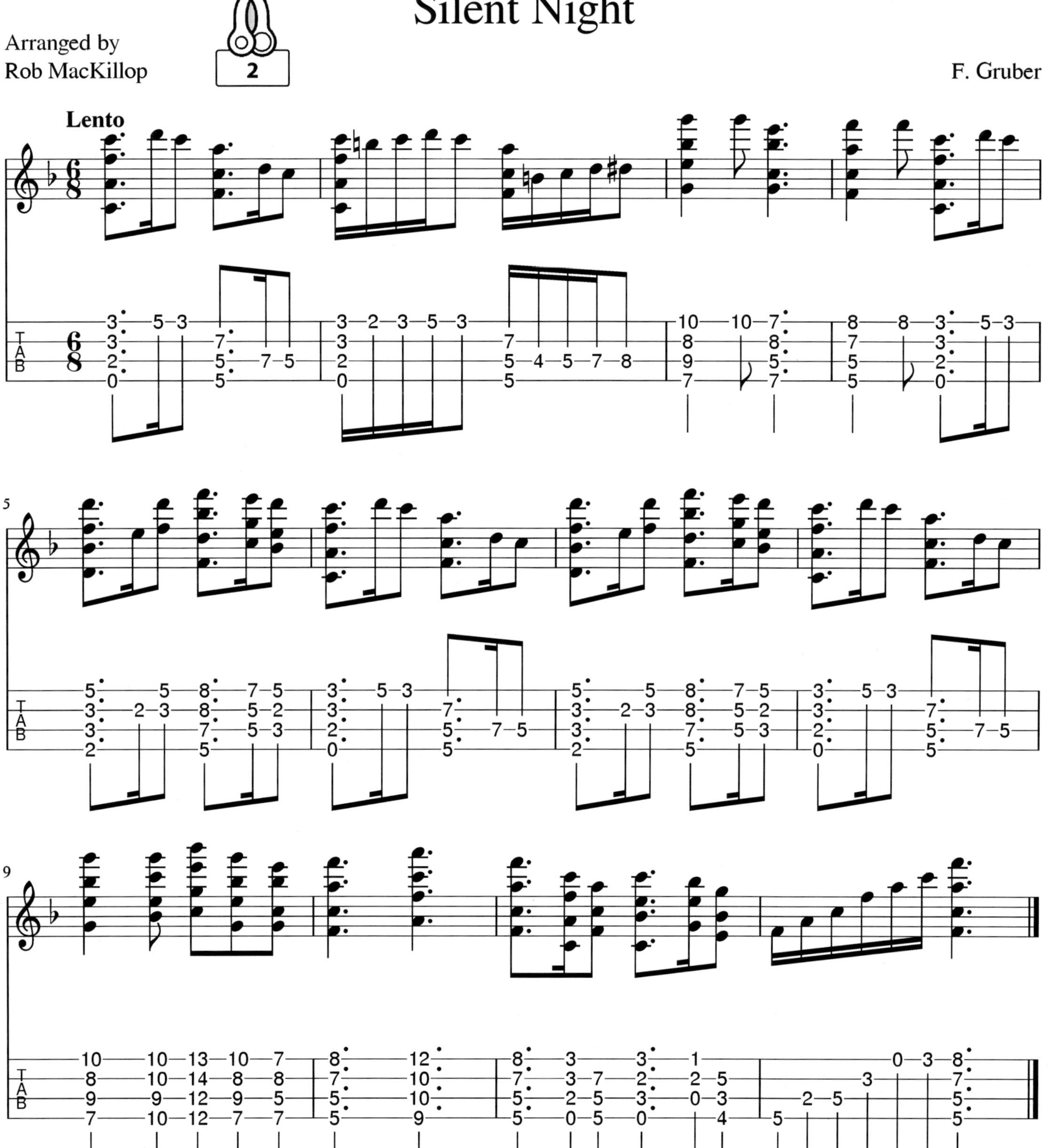

Auld Lang Syne

Arranged by
Rob MacKillop

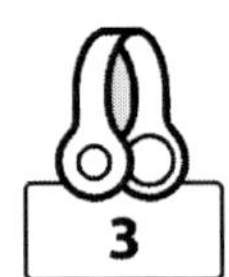

Arrangement in memoriam,
Eddy Davis 'The Manhattan Minstrel'

Traditional Scots

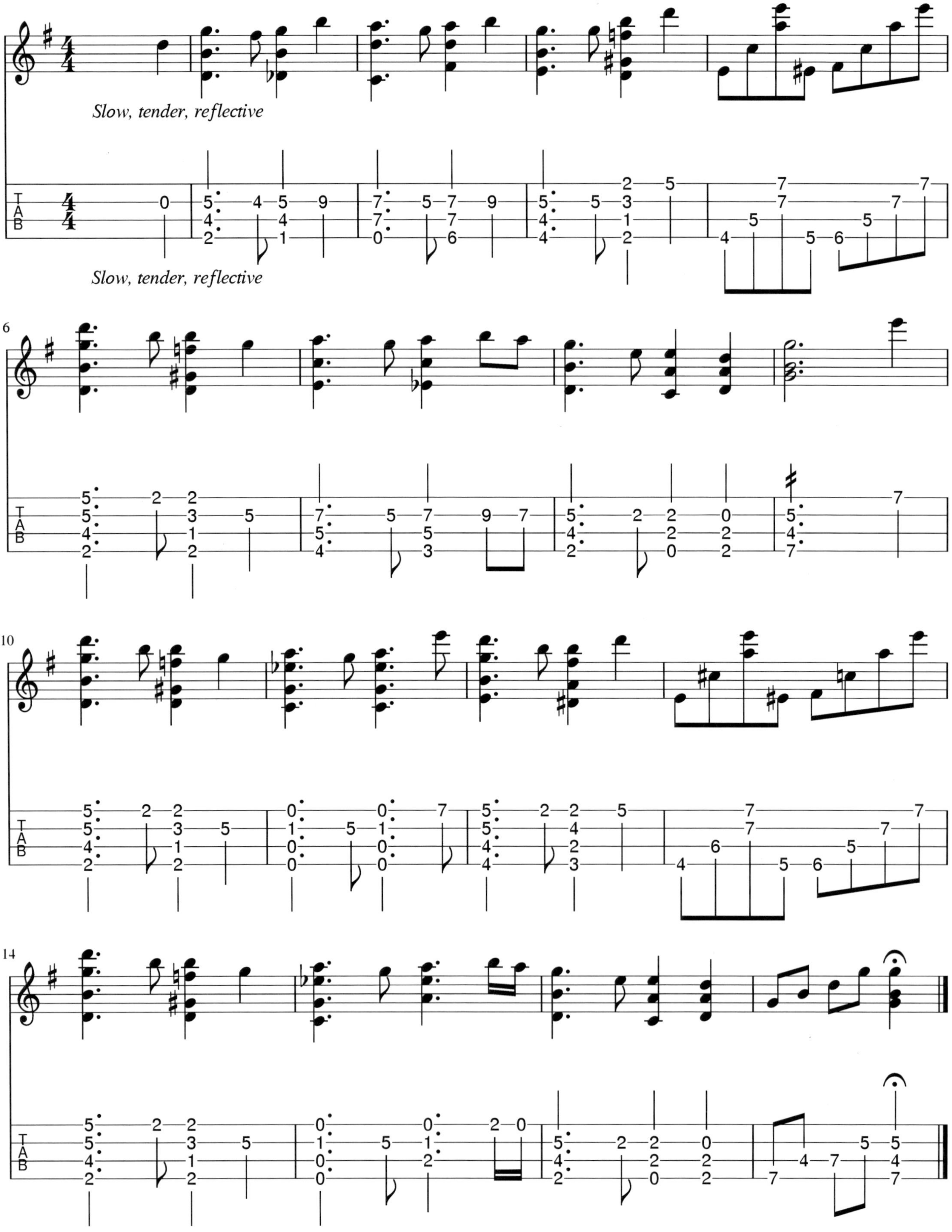

Slow, tender, reflective

Slow, tender, reflective

6

10

14

Ding Dong Merrily on High

Arranged by
Rob MacKillop

4

Anon. French Medieval

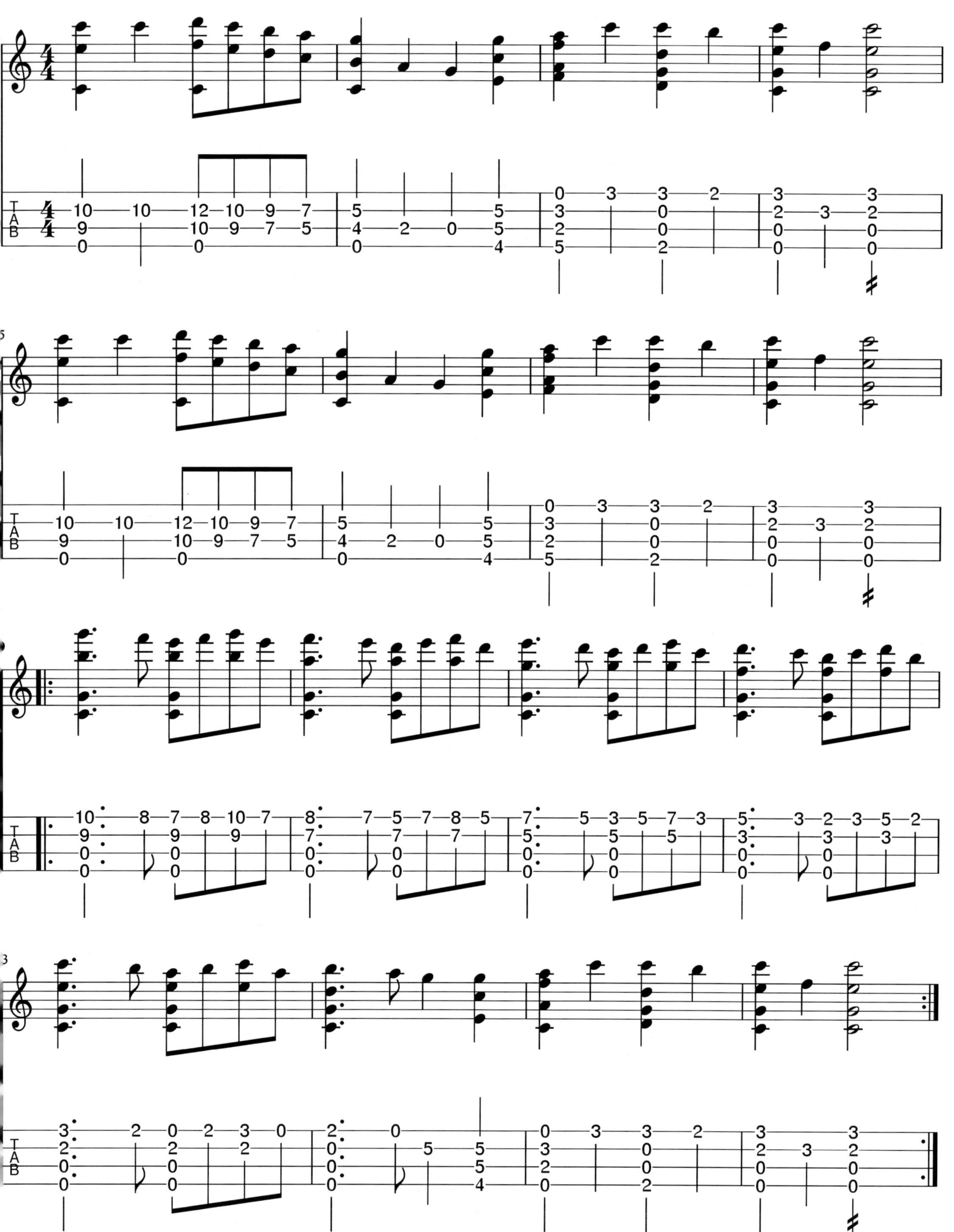

O Christmas Tree

Arranged by
Rob MacKillop

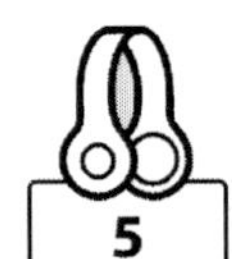

E. Anschutz

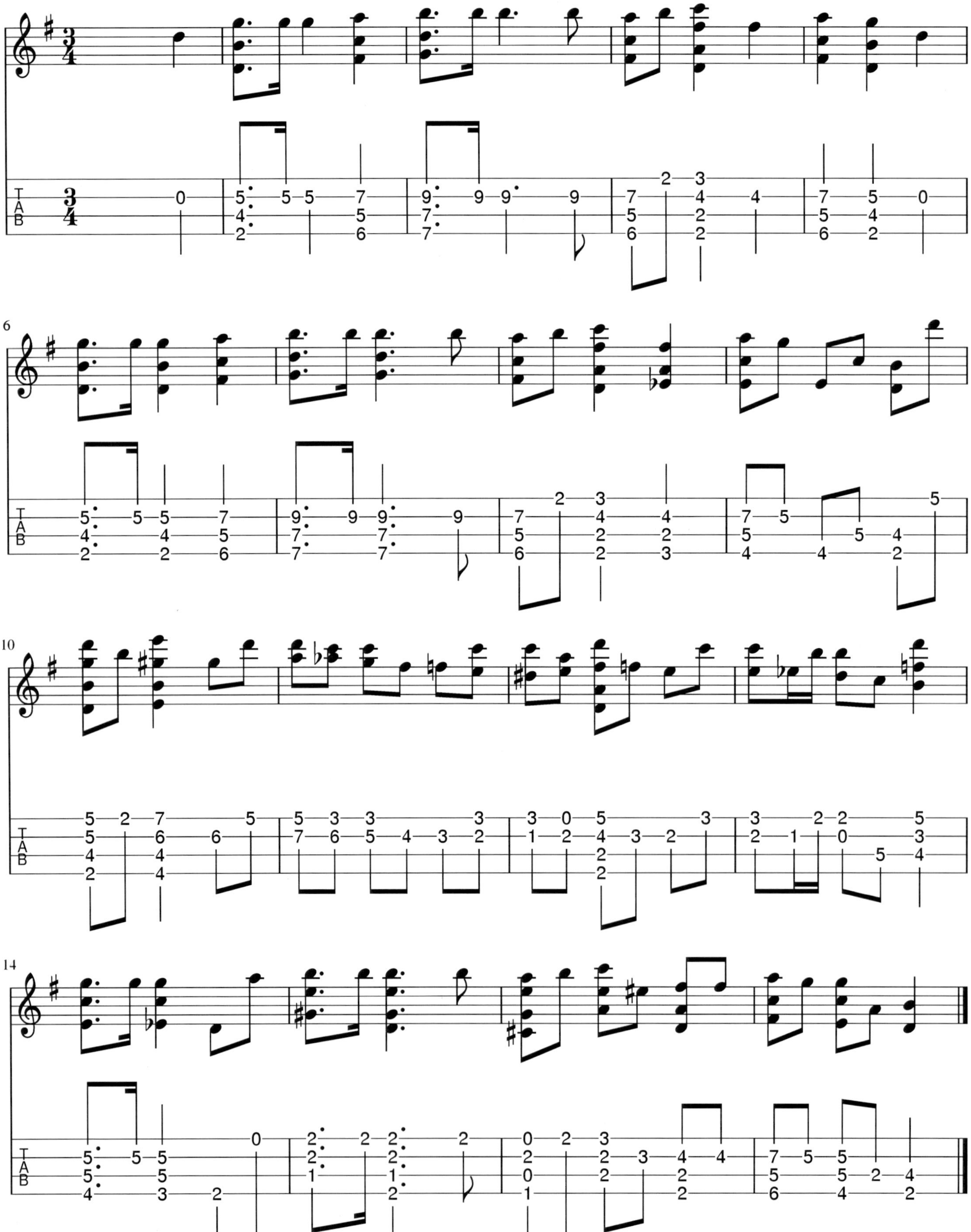

This page has been left blank to avoid an awkward page turn.

I Saw Three Ships

Arranged by
Rob MacKillop

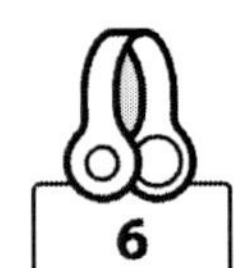

Traditional English Carol

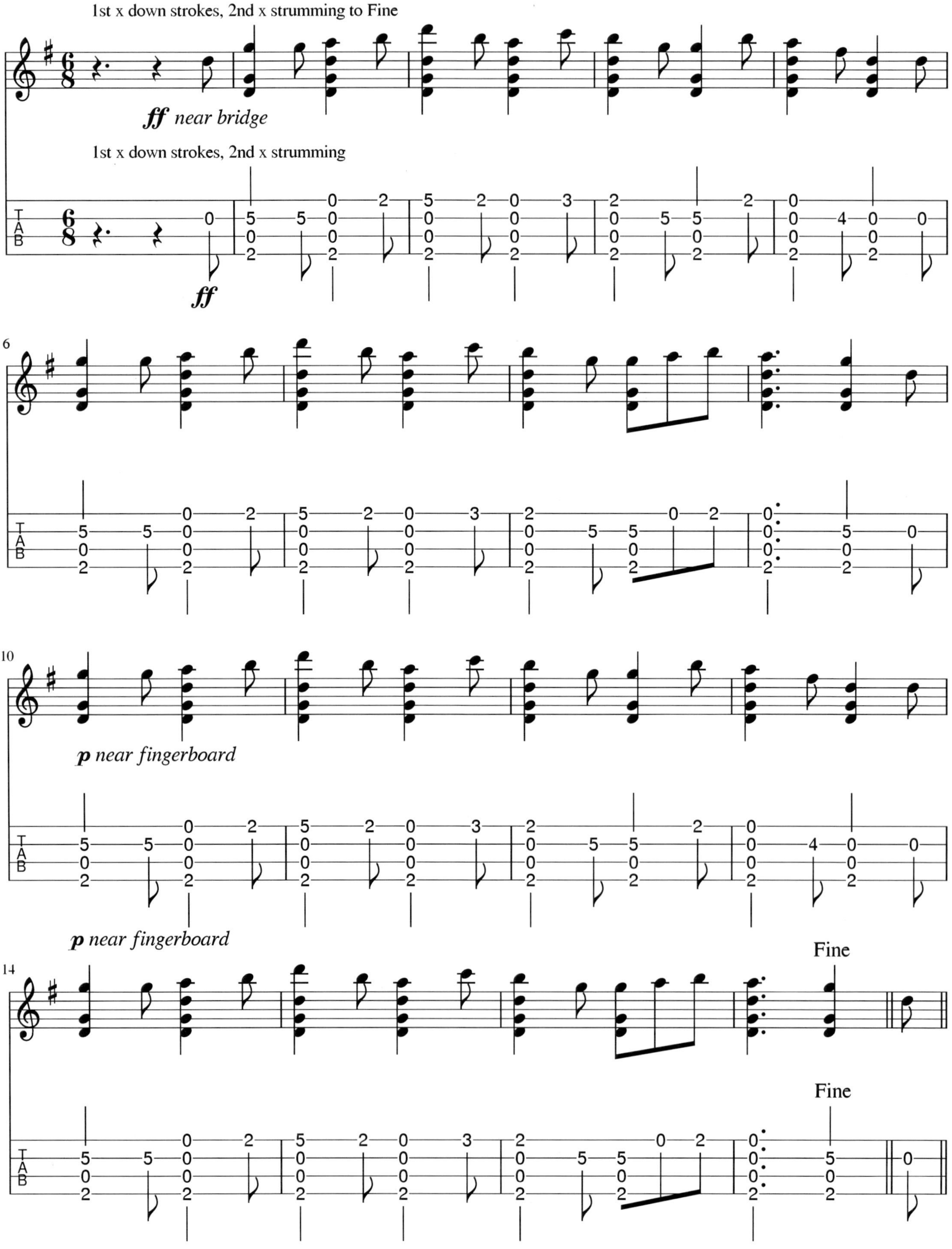

1st x down strokes, 2nd x strumming to Fine

ff near bridge

1st x down strokes, 2nd x strumming

ff

6

10

p near fingerboard

p near fingerboard

14

Fine

Fine

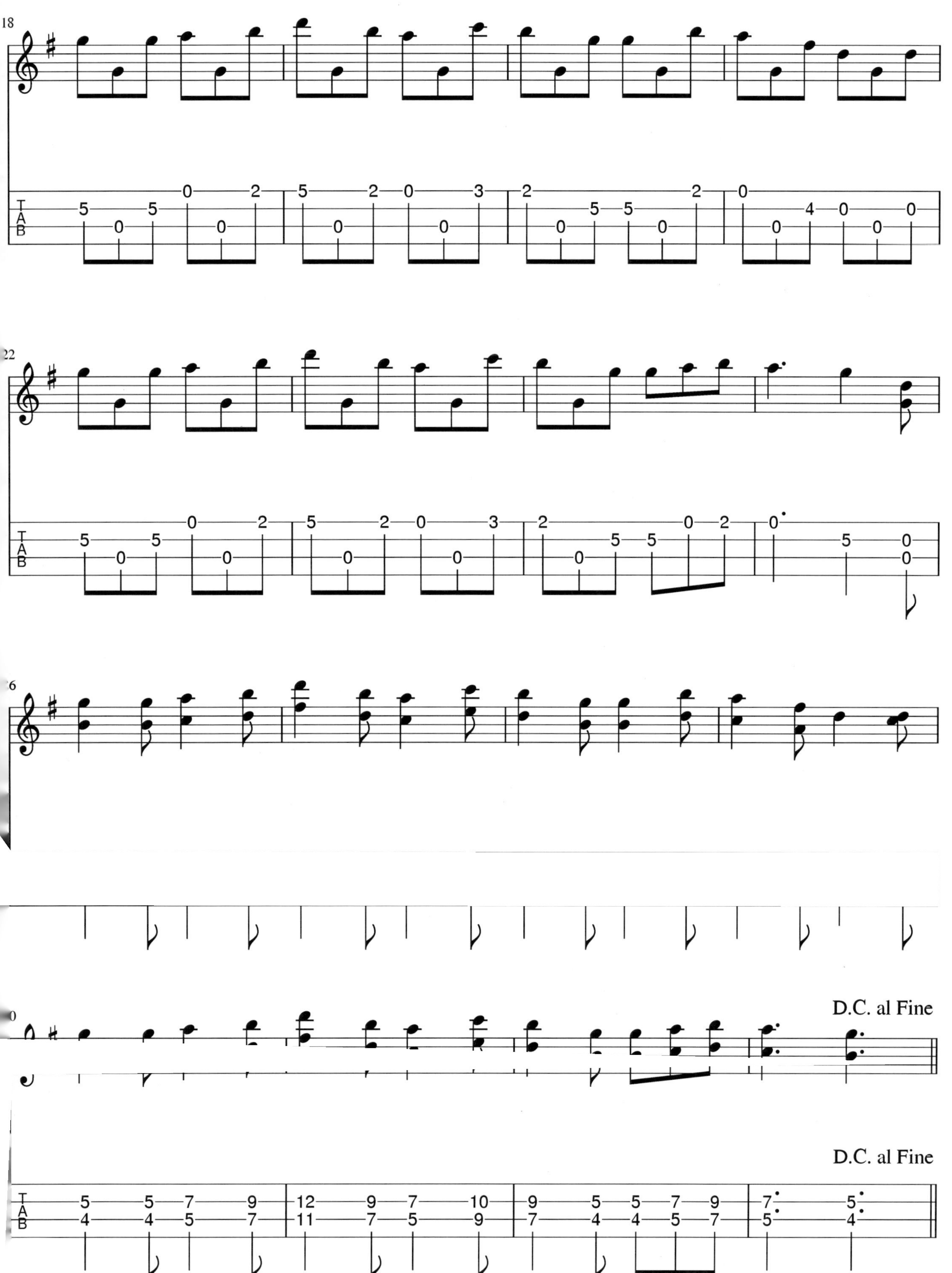
D.C. al Fine
D.C. al Fine

In the Bleak Midwinter

Arranged by
Rob MacKillop

G. Holst

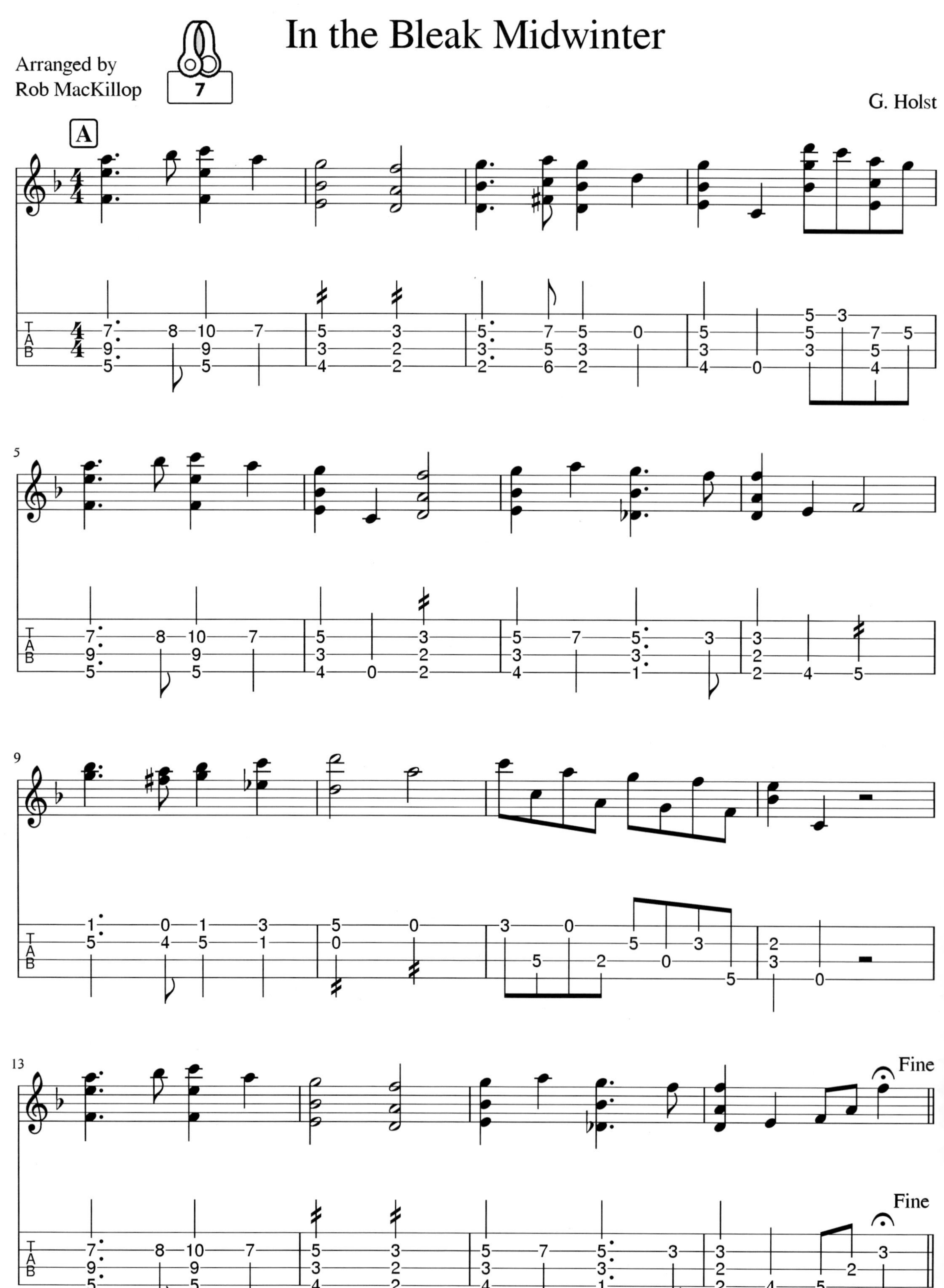

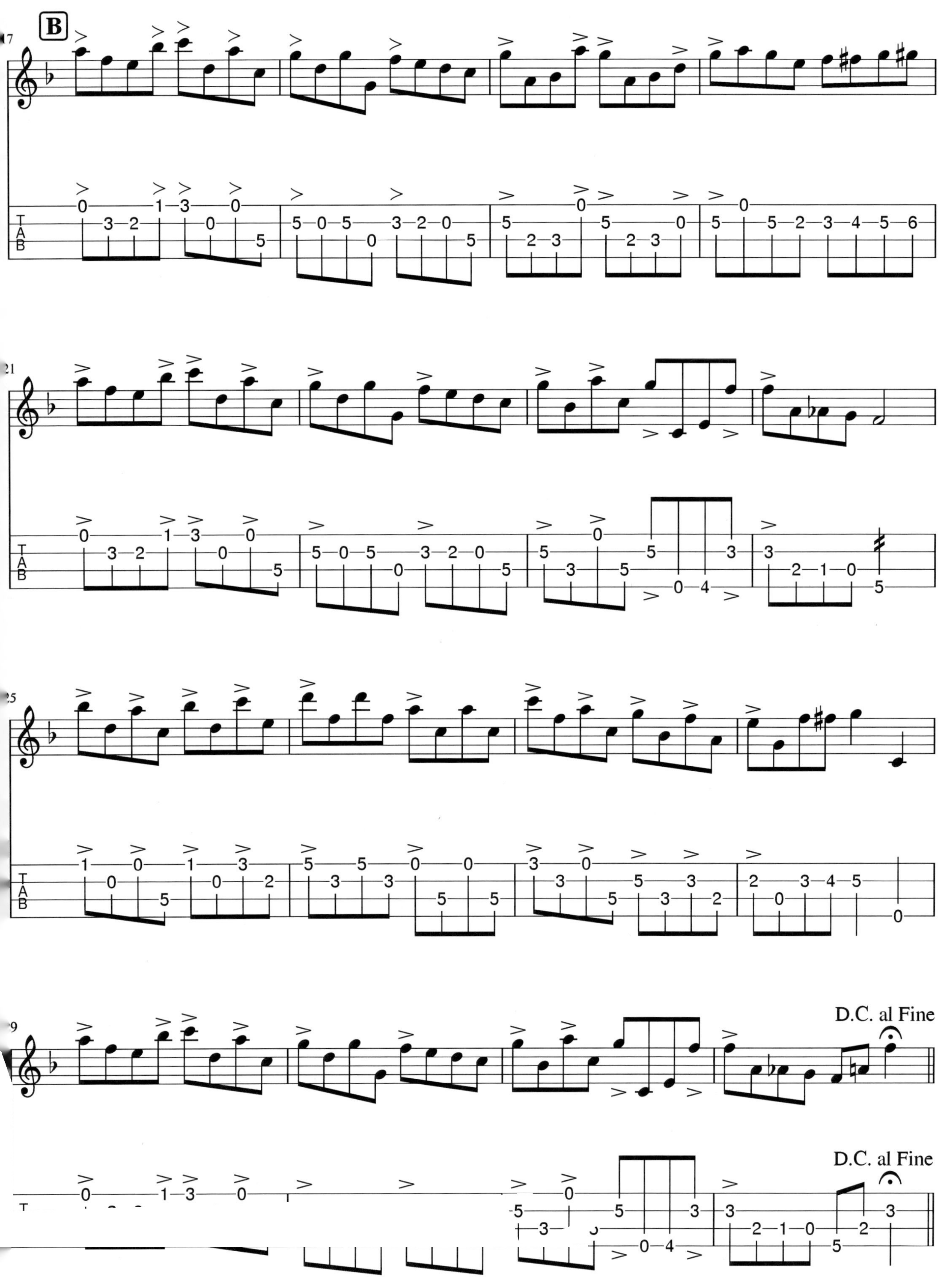
B
17
21
25
29
D.C. al Fine
D.C. al Fine

The Coventry Carol

"Lully, lullay, thou little tiny child"

Arranged by
Rob MacKillop

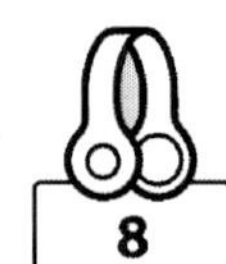

Traditional English Carol

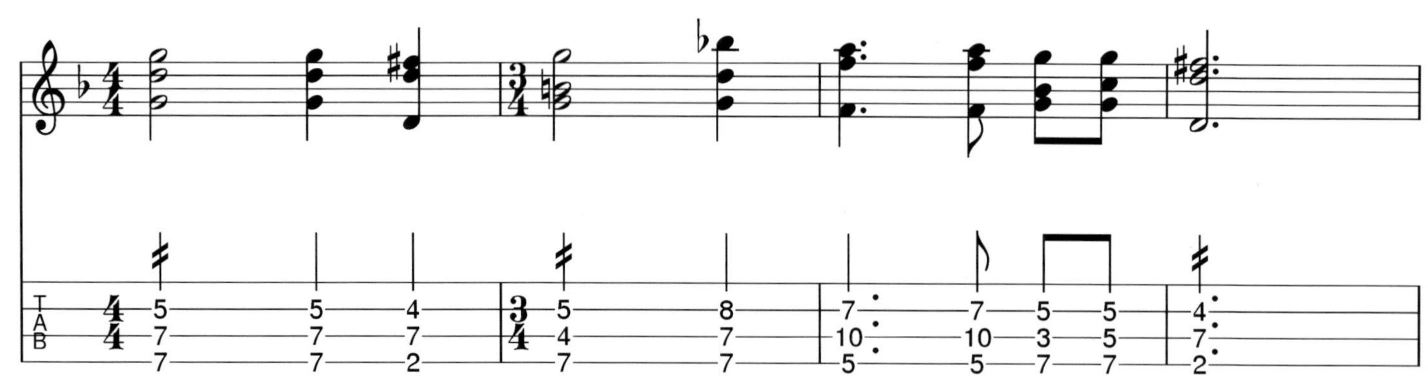

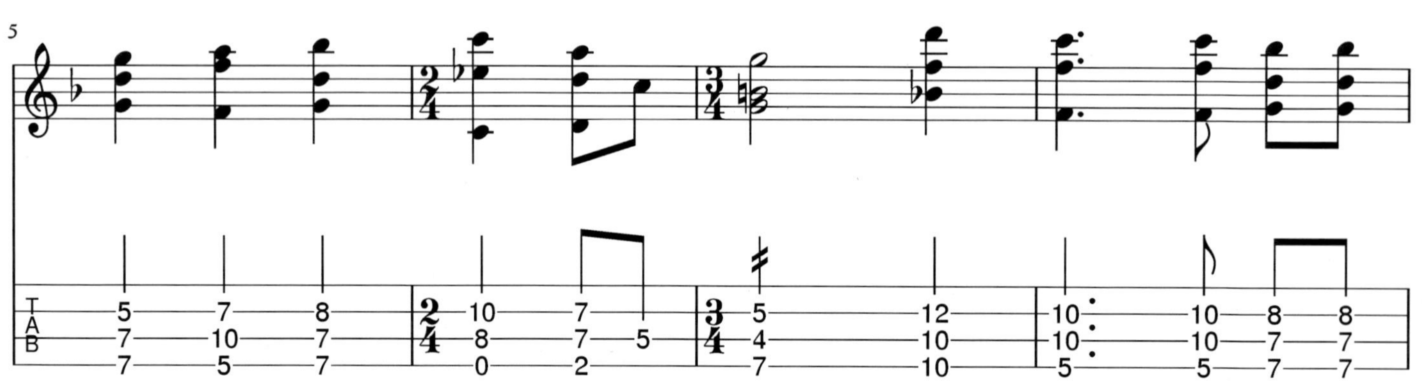

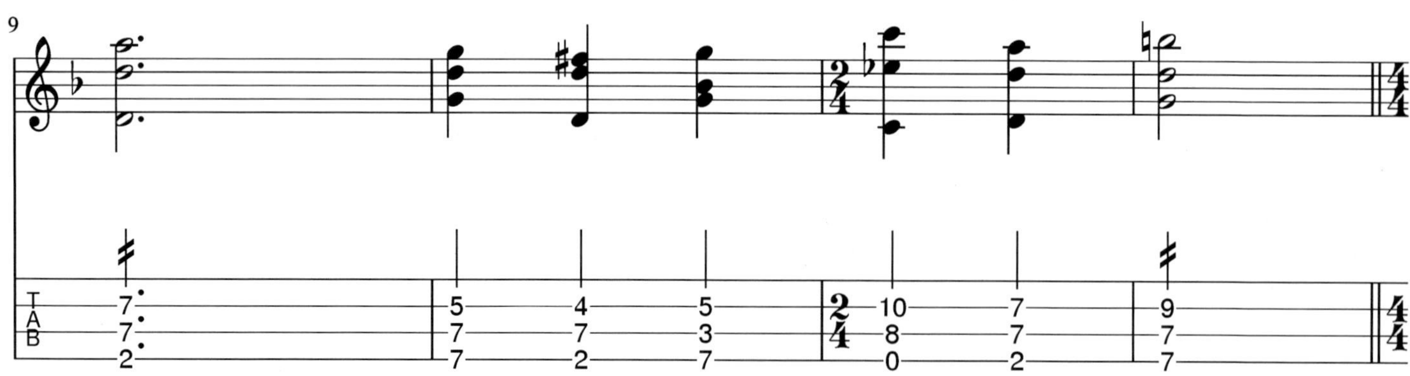

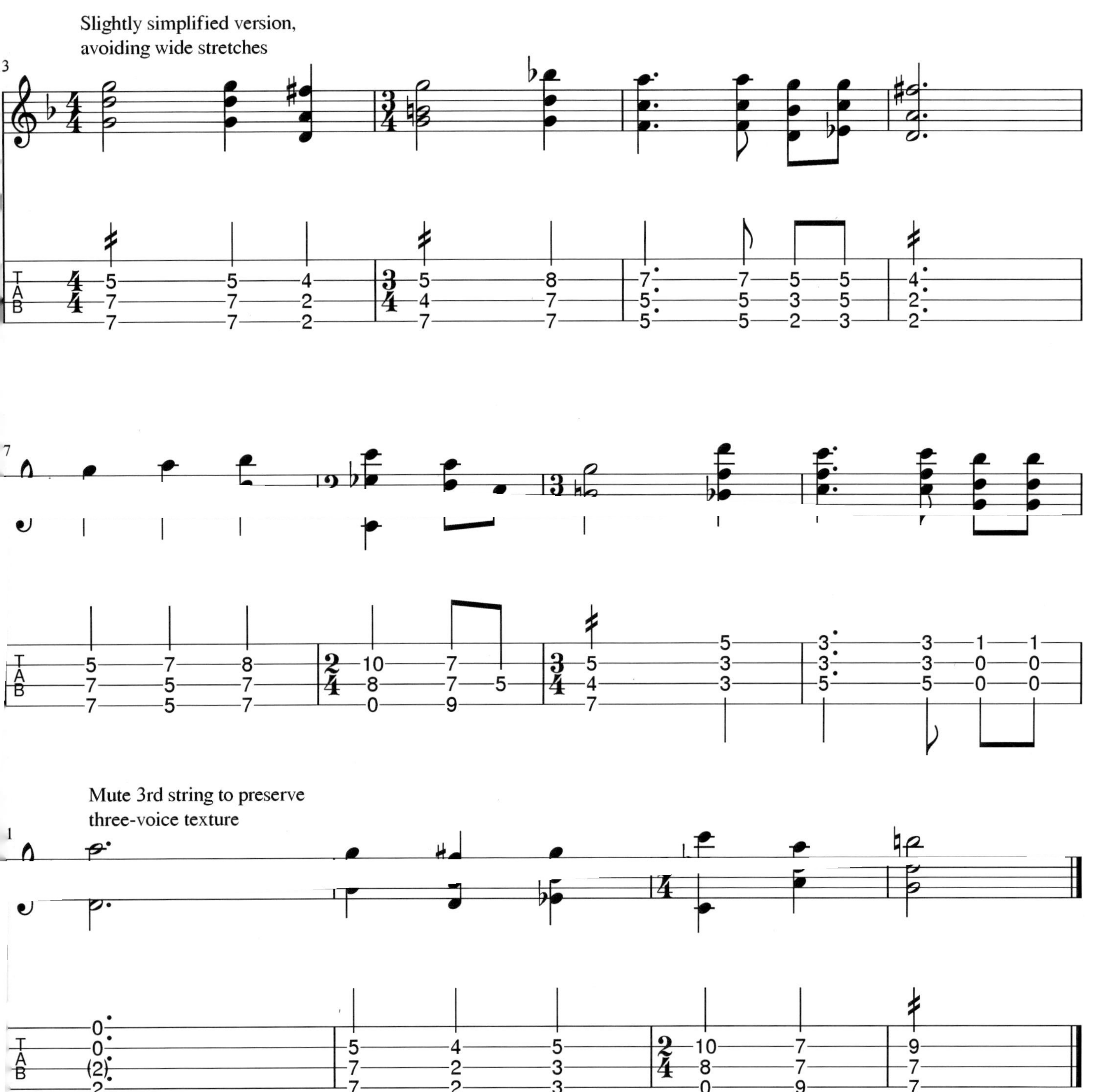
Slightly simplified version,
avoiding wide stretches
Mute 3rd string to preserve
three-voice texture

Once in Royal David's City

Arranged by
Rob MacKillop

H. J. Gauntlet

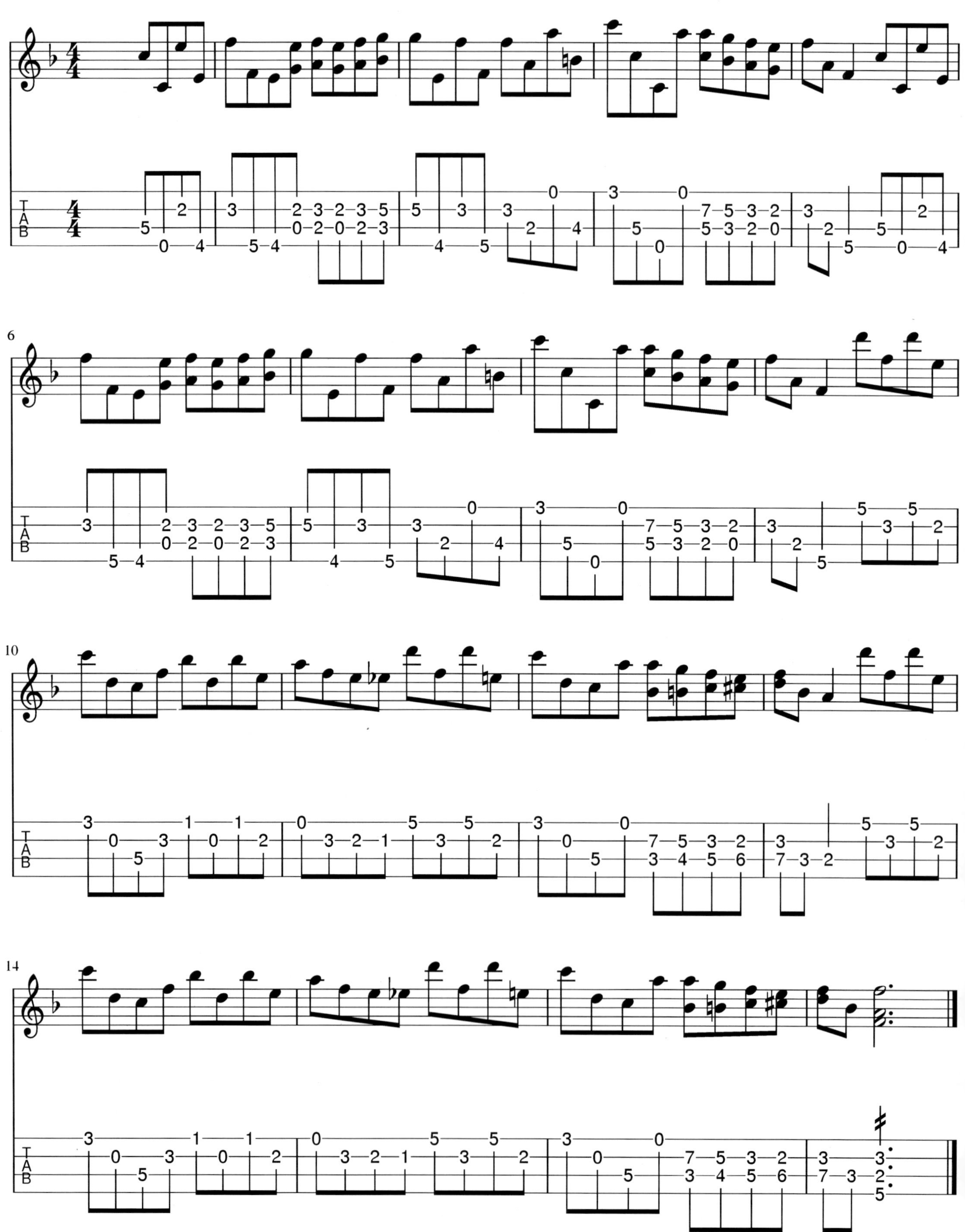

Arranged by
Rob MacKillop

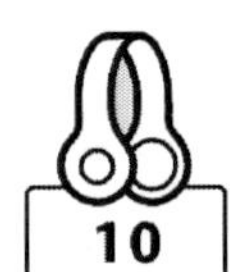

What Child Is This?

To the tune of "Greensleeves"

Traditional

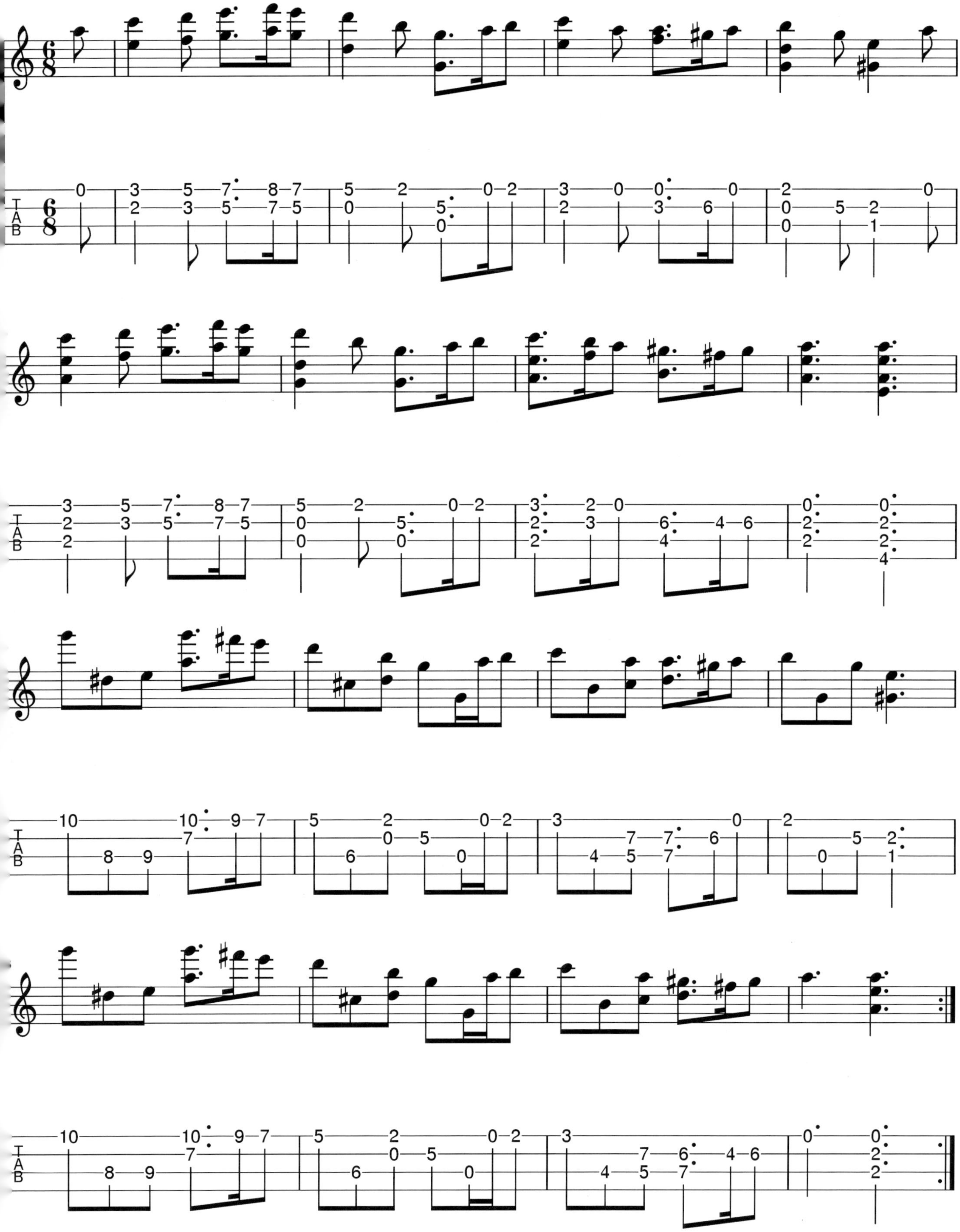

Gaudete

16th-Century Finnish/Swedish

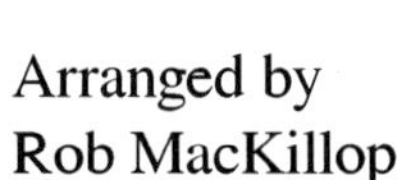

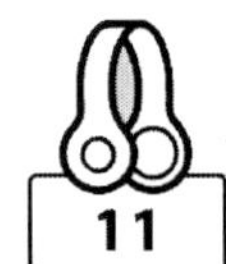

Anon.

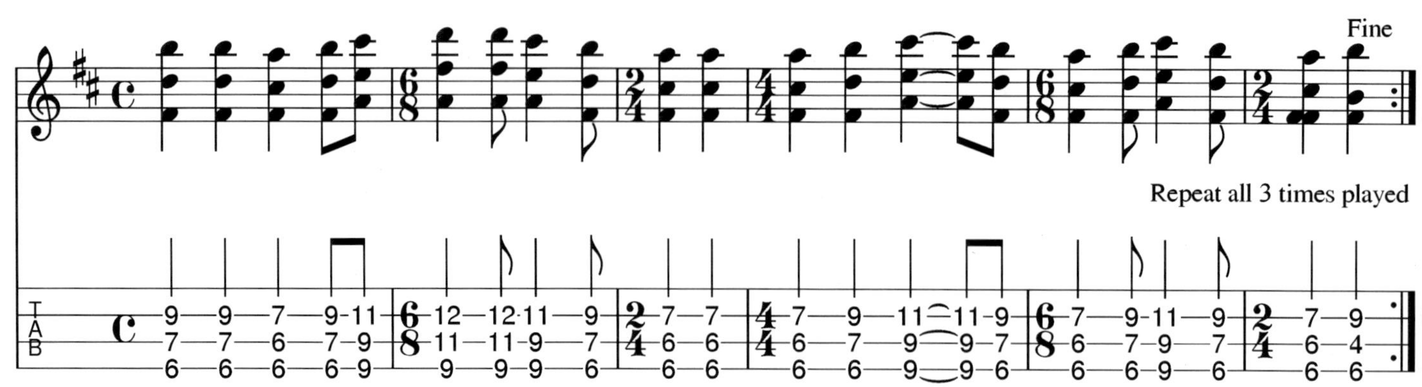

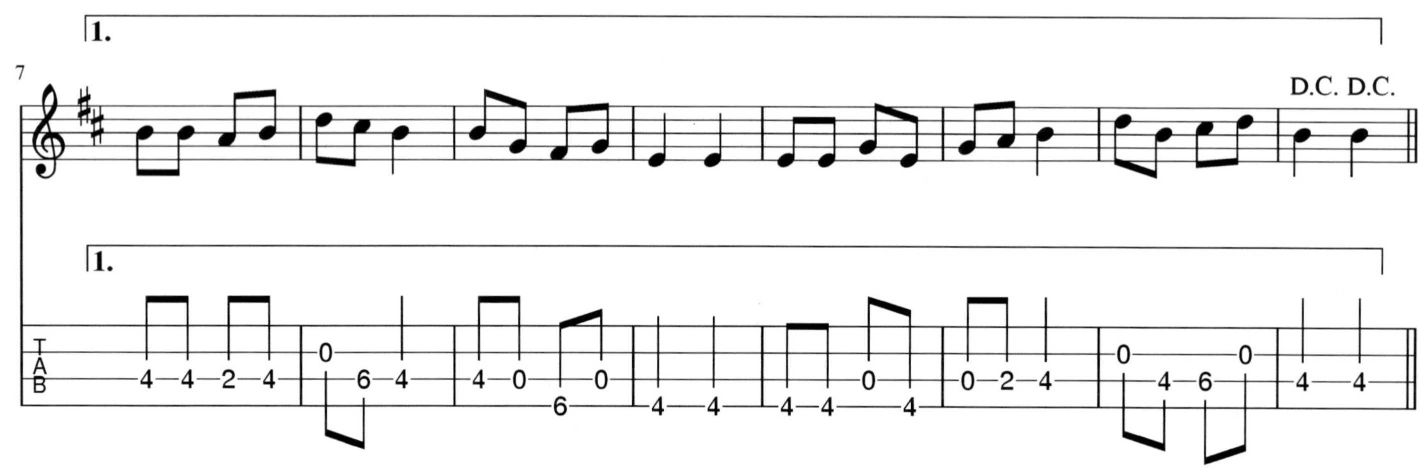

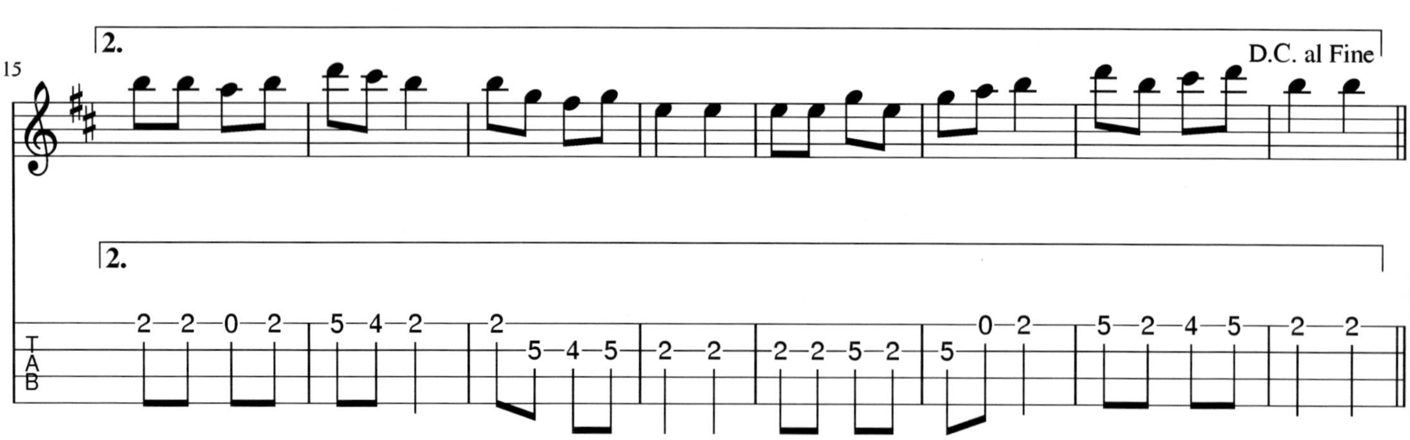

Cuncti Simus

Medieval Catalan

Arranged by
Rob MacKillop

Llibre Vermell
de Montserrat

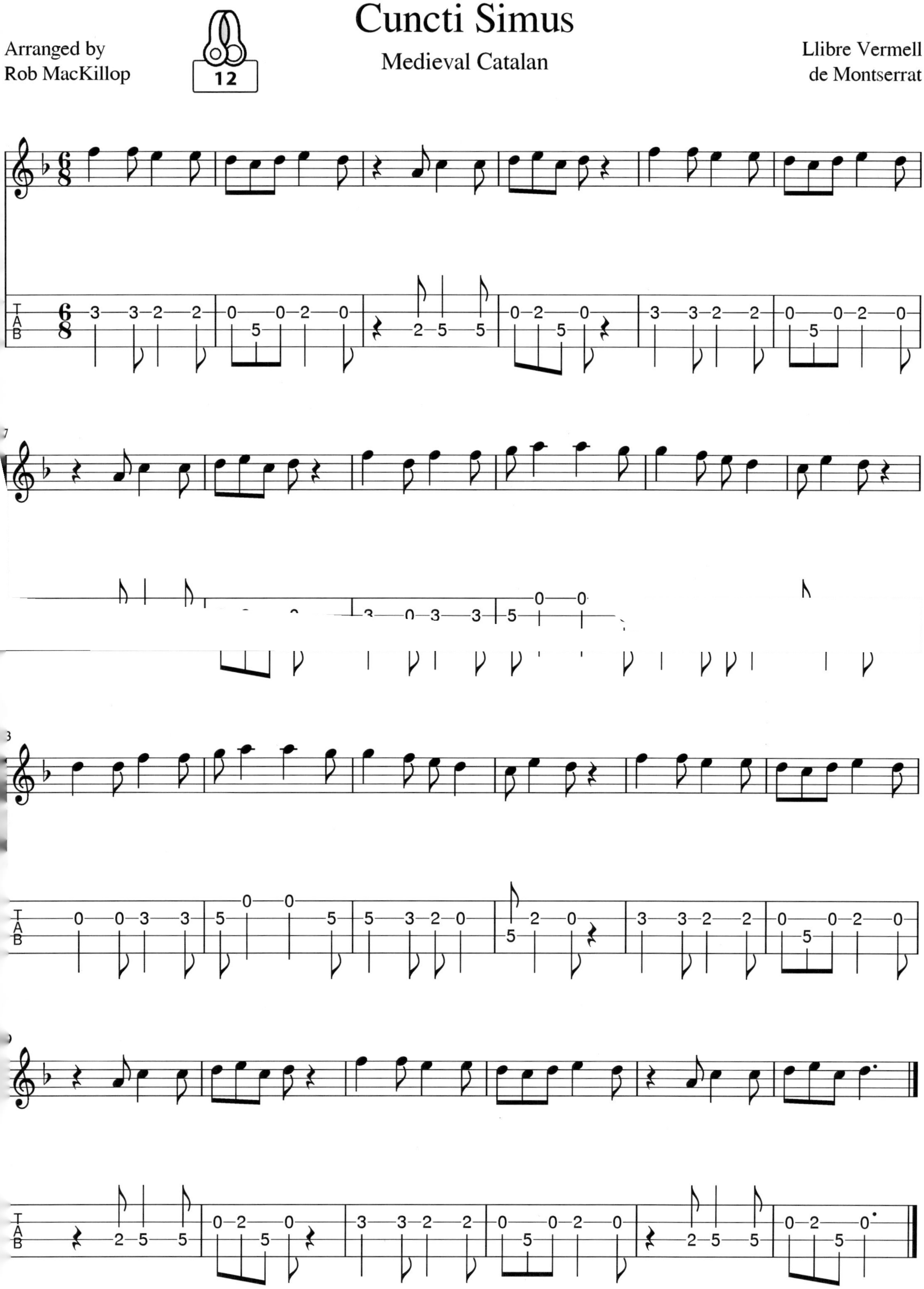

Los Sept Goyts

Medieval Catalan

Arranged by
Rob MacKillop

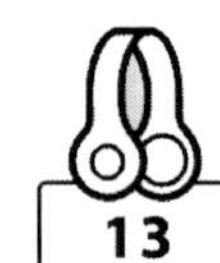

Llibre Vermell
de Montserrat

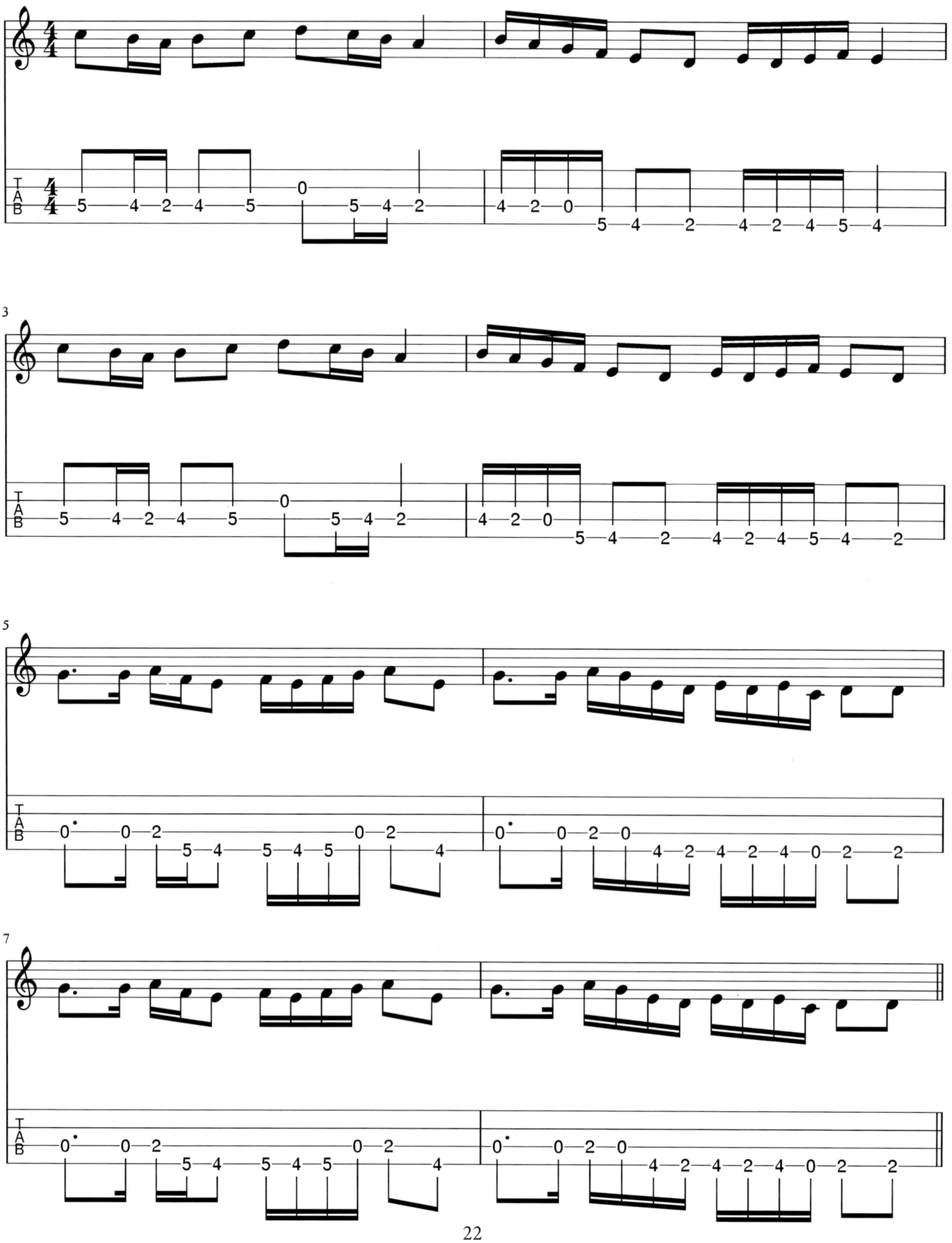

3

5

7

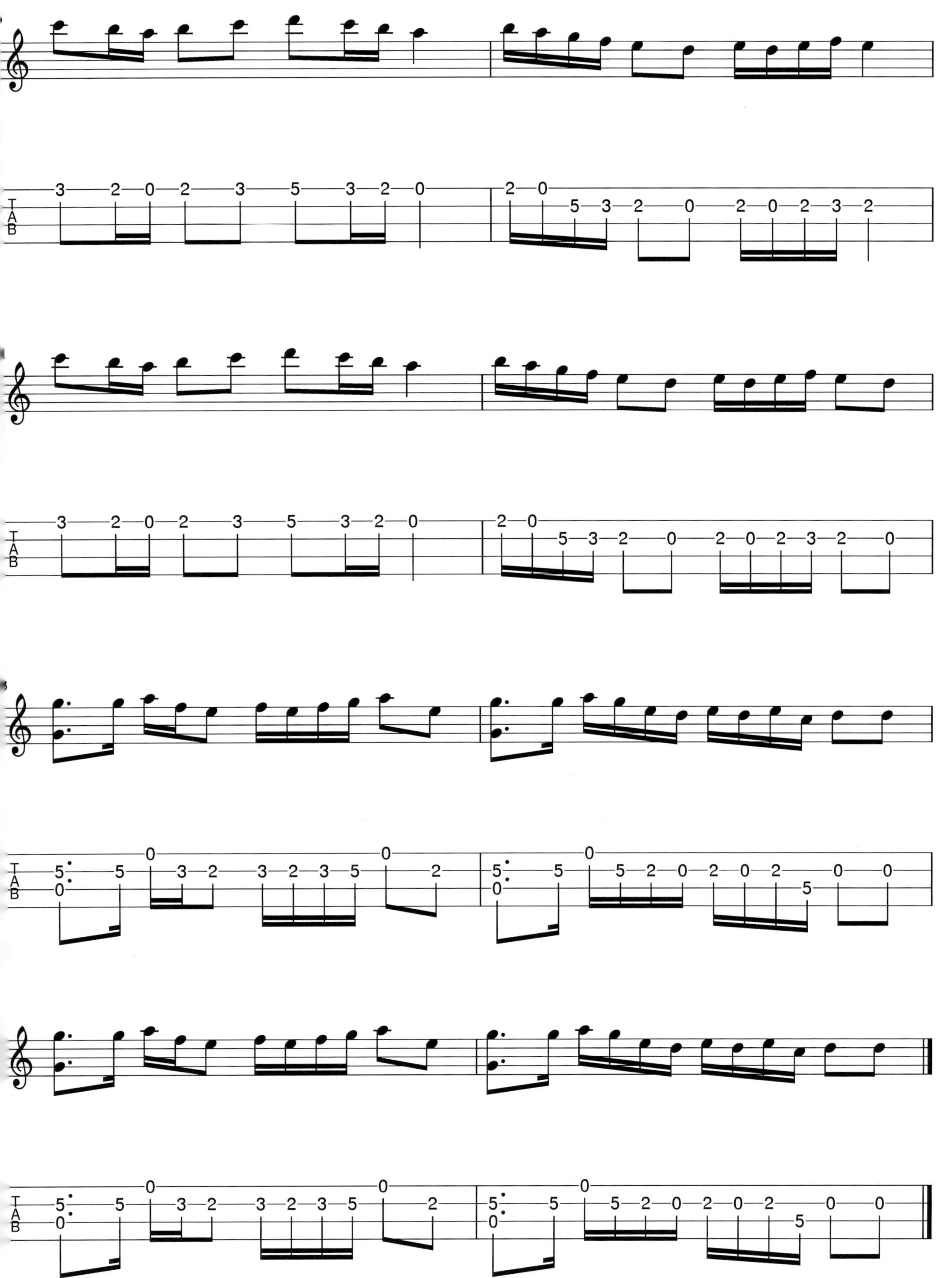
T
A
B

Rosa das rosas

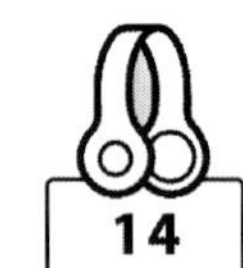

Arranged by
Rob MacKillop

Medieval Spanish

Cantigas de Santa Maria

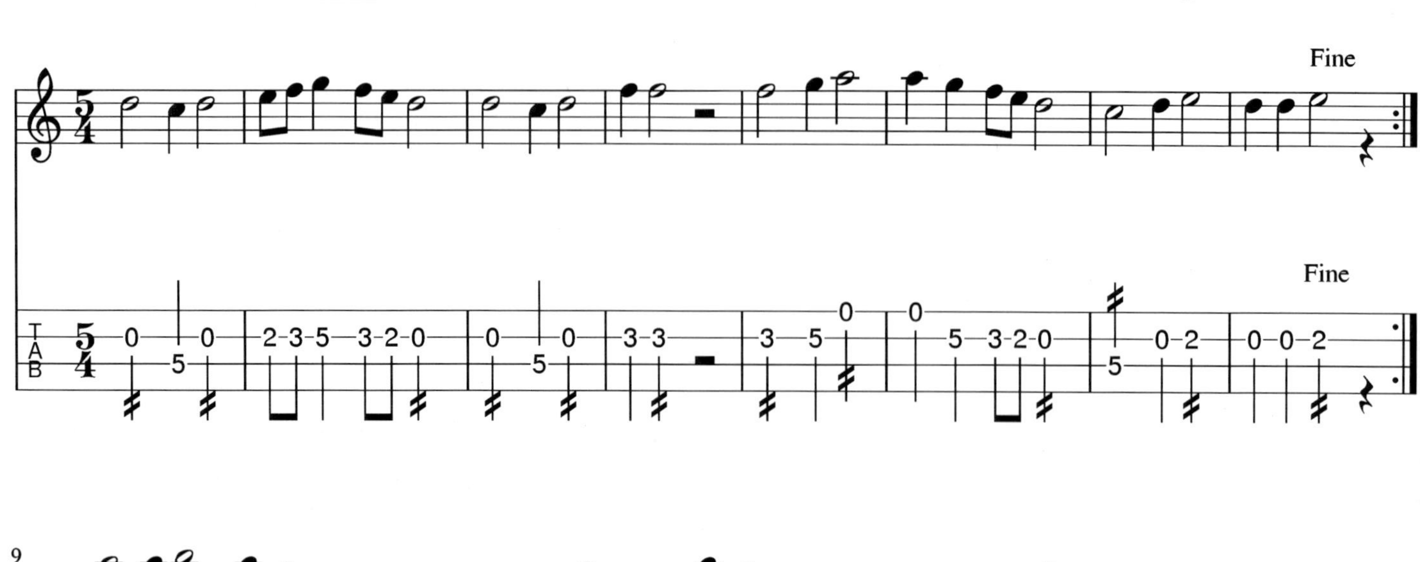

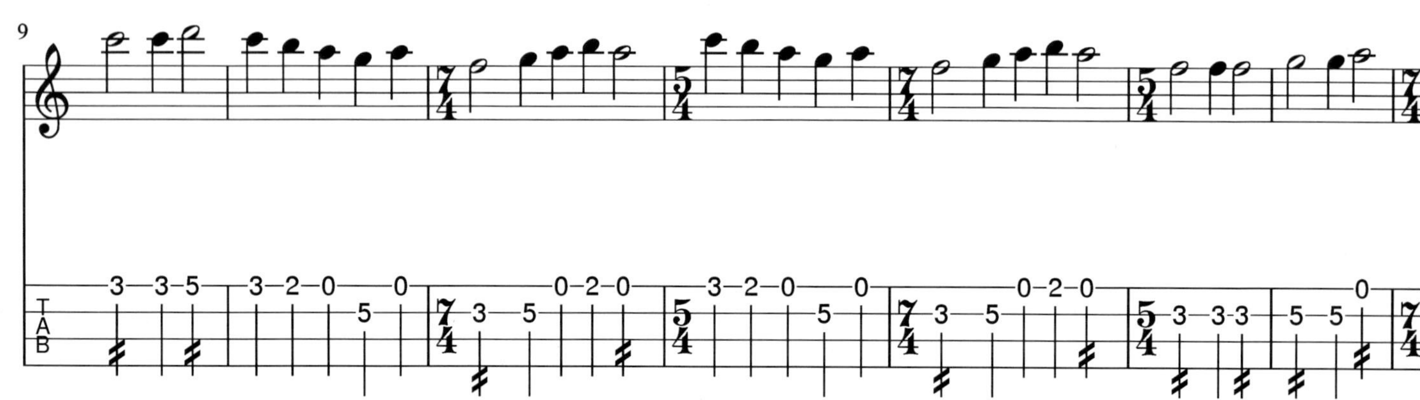

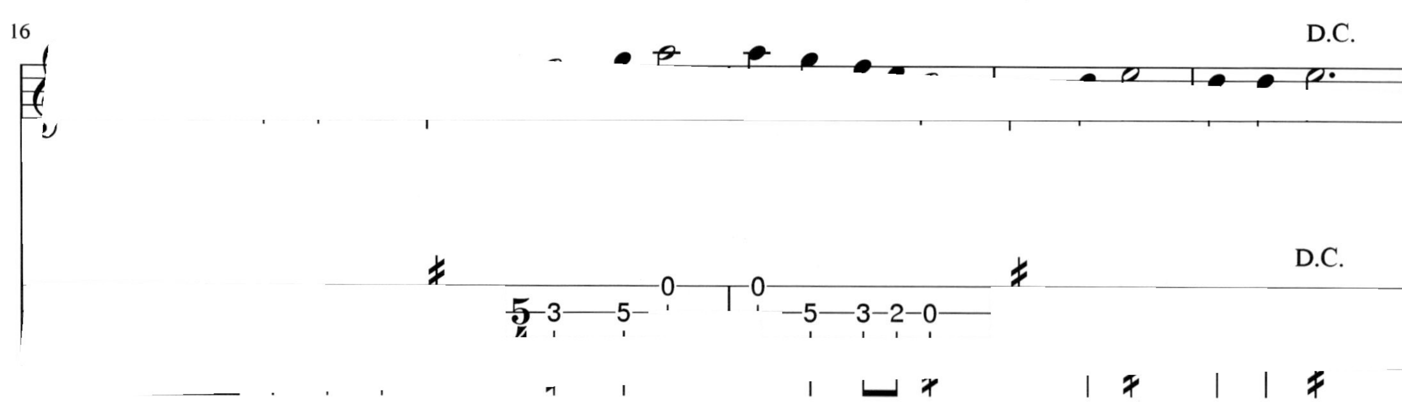